THE
LITTLE BOOK OF
SELF-CARE
— FOR —
TAURUS

*Simple Ways to Refresh
and Restore—According
to the Stars*

CONSTANCE STELLAS

ADAMS MEDIA

NEW YORK LONDON TORONTO SYDNEY NEW DELHI

Adams Media
An Imprint of Simon & Schuster, Inc.
100 Technology Center Drive
Stoughton, MA 02072

First Adams Media hardcover edition January 2019

ADAMS MEDIA and colophon are trademarks of Simon & Schuster.

For information about special discounts for bulk purchases,
please contact Simon & Schuster Special Sales at 1-866-506-1949
or business@simonandschuster.com.

The Simon & Schuster Speakers Bureau can bring authors to your live event. For
more information or to book an event contact the Simon & Schuster Speakers
Bureau at 1-866-248-3049 or visit our website at www.simonspeakers.com.

Interior design by Colleen Cunningham
Interior images © Getty Images; Clipart.com

Manufactured in the United States of America

5 2021

Library of Congress Cataloging-in-Publication Data has been applied for.

ISBN 978-1-5072-0966-0
ISBN 978-1-5072-0967-7 (ebook)

Dedication

To my kind, salt-of-the-earth Taurus sister,
Kristina, with love.

CONTENTS

Acknowledgments

I would like to thank Karen Cooper and everyone at Adams Media who helped with this book. To Brendan O'Neill, Katie Corcoran Lytle, Sarah Doughty, Eileen Mullan, Laura Daly, Brett Palana-Shanahan, Julia Jacques, Casey Ebert, Sylvia Davis, and everyone else who worked on the manuscripts. To Frank Rivera, Colleen Cunningham, and Katrina Machado for their work on the book's cover and interior design. I appreciated your team spirit and eagerness to dive into the riches of astrology.

Introduction

It's time for you to have a little *"me" time*—powered by the zodiac. By tapping into your Sun sign's astrological and elemental energies, *The Little Book of Self-Care for Taurus* brings star-powered strength and cosmic relief to your life with self-care guidance tailored specifically for you.

While you may enjoy observing the world from a safe distance, Taurus, this book focuses on your true self. This book provides information on how to incorporate self-care into your life while teaching you just how important astrology is to your overall self-care routine. You'll learn more about yourself as you learn about your sign and its governing element, earth. Then you can relax, rejuvenate, and stay balanced with more than one hundred self-care ideas and activities perfect for your Taurus personality.

From meditating with rose quartz to indulging in a sweet treat, you will find plenty of ways to heal your mind, body, and active spirit. Now, let the stars be your self-care guide!

PART 1

SIGNS, ELEMENTS, AND SELF-CARE

CHAPTER 1
WHAT IS SELF-CARE?

✳

Astrology gives insights into whom to love, when to charge forward into new beginnings, and how to succeed in whatever you put your mind to. When paired with self-care, astrology can also help you relax and reclaim that part of yourself that tends to get lost in the bustle of the day. In this chapter you'll learn what self-care is—for you. (No matter your sign, self-care is more than just lit candles and quiet reflection, though these activities may certainly help you find the renewal that you seek.) You'll also learn how making a priority of personalized self-care activities can benefit you in ways you may not even have thought of. Whether you're a Leo, a Pisces, or a Taurus, you deserve rejuvenation and renewal that's customized to your sign—this chapter reveals where to begin.

What Self-Care Is

Self-care is any activity that you do to take care of yourself. It rejuvenates your body, refreshes your mind, or realigns your spirit. It relaxes and refuels you. It gets you ready for a new day or a fresh start. It's the practices, rituals, and meaningful activities that you do, just for you, that help you feel safe, grounded, happy, and fulfilled.

The activities that qualify as self-care are amazingly unique and personalized to who you are, what you like, and, in large part, what your astrological sign is. If you're asking questions about what self-care practices are best for those ruled by earth and born under the practical eye of Taurus, you'll find answers—and restoration—in Part 2. But, no matter which of those self-care activities speak to you and your unique place in the universe on any given day, it will fall into one of the following self-care categories—each of which pertains to a different aspect of your life:

* Physical self-care
* Emotional self-care
* Social self-care
* Mental self-care
* Spiritual self-care
* Practical self-care

When you practice all of these unique types of self-care—and prioritize your practice to ensure you are choosing the best options for your unique sign and governing element—know that you are actively working to create the version of yourself that the universe intends you to be.

Physical Self-Care

When you practice physical self-care, you make the decision to look after and restore the one physical body that has been bestowed upon you. Care for it. Use it in the best way you can imagine, for that is what the universe wishes you to do. You can't light the world on fire or move mountains if you're not doing everything you can to take care of your physical health.

Emotional Self-Care

Emotional self-care is when you take the time to acknowledge and care for your inner self, your emotional well-being. Whether you're angry or frustrated, happy or joyful, or somewhere in between, emotional self-care happens when you choose to sit with your emotions: when you step away from the noise of daily life that often drowns out or tamps down your authentic self. Emotional self-care lets you see your inner you as the cosmos intend. Once you identify your true emotions, you can either accept them and continue to move forward on your journey or you can try to change any negative emotions for the better. The more you acknowledge your feelings and practice emotional self-care, the more you'll feel the positivity that the universe and your life holds for you.

Social Self-Care

You practice social self-care when you nurture your relationships with others, be they friends, coworkers, or family members. In today's hectic world it's easy to let relationships fall to the wayside, but it's so important to share your life with others—and let others share their lives with you. Social self-care is reciprocal and often karmic. The support and love that you put out into the universe through social self-care is given back to you by those you socialize with—often tenfold.

Mental Self-Care

Mental self-care is anything that keeps your mind working quickly and critically. It helps you cut through the fog of the day, week, or year and ensures that your quick wit and sharp mind are intact and working the way the cosmos intended. Making sure your mind is fit helps you problem-solve, decreases stress since you're not feeling overwhelmed, and keeps you feeling on top of your mental game—no matter your sign or your situation.

Spiritual Self-Care

Spiritual self-care is self-care that allows you to tap into your soul and the soul of the universe and uncover its secrets. Rather than focusing on a particular religion or set of religious beliefs, these types of self-care activities reconnect you with a higher power: the sense that something out there is bigger than you. When you meditate, you connect. When you pray, you connect. Whenever you do something that allows you to experience and marry yourself to the vastness that is the cosmos, you practice spiritual self-care.

Practical Self-Care

Self-care is what you do to take care of yourself, and practical self-care, while not as expansive as the other types, is made up of the seemingly small day-to-day tasks that bring you peace and accomplishment. These practical self-care rituals are important, but are often overlooked. Scheduling a doctor's appointment that you've been putting off is practical self-care. Getting your hair cut is practical self-care. Anything you can check off your list of things to be accomplished gives you a sacred space to breathe and allows the universe more room to bring a beautiful sense of cosmic fulfillment your way.

What Self-Care Isn't

Self-care is restorative. Self-care is clarifying. Self-care is whatever you need to do to make yourself feel secure in the universe.

Now that you know what self-care is, it's also important that you're able to see what self-care isn't. Self-care is not something that you force yourself to do because you think it will be good for you. Some signs are energy in motion and sitting still goes against their place in the universe. Those signs won't feel refreshed by lying in a hammock or sitting down to meditate. Other signs aren't able to ground themselves unless they've found a self-care practice that protects their cosmic need for peace and quiet. Those signs won't find parties, concerts, and loud venues soothing or satisfying. If a certain ritual doesn't bring you peace, clarity, or satisfaction, then it's not right for your sign and you should find something that speaks to you more clearly.

There's a difference though between not finding satisfaction in a ritual that you've tried and not wanting to try a self-care activity because you're tired or stuck in a comfort zone. Sometimes going to the gym or meeting up with friends is the self-care practice that you need to experience—whether engaging in it feels like a downer or not. So consider how you feel when you're actually doing the activity. If it feels invigorating to get on the treadmill or you feel delight when you actually catch up with your friend, the ritual is doing what it should be doing and clearing space for you—among other benefits...

The Benefits of Self-Care

The benefits of self-care are boundless and there's none that's superior to helping you put rituals in place to feel more at home in your body, in your spirit, and in your unique home in the cosmos. There are, however, other benefits to engaging in the practice of self-care that you should know.

Rejuvenates Your Immune System

No matter which rituals are designated for you by the stars, your sign, and its governing element, self-care helps both your body and mind rest, relax, and recuperate. The practice of self-care activates the parasympathetic nervous system (often called the rest and digest system), which slows your heart rate, calms the body, and overall helps your body relax and release tension. This act of decompression gives your body the space it needs to build up and strengthen your immune system, which protects you from illness.

Helps You Reconnect—with Yourself

When you practice the ritual of self-care—especially when you customize this practice based on your personal sign and governing element—you learn what you like to do and what you need to do to replenish yourself. Knowing yourself better, and allowing yourself the time and space that you need to focus on your personal needs and desires, gives you the gifts of self-confidence and self-knowledge. Setting time aside to focus on your needs also helps you put busy, must-do things aside, which gives you time to reconnect with yourself and who you are deep inside.

Increases Compassion

Perhaps one of the most important benefits of creating a self-care ritual is that, by focusing on yourself, you become more compassionate to others as well. When you truly take the time to care for yourself and make yourself and your importance in the universe a priority in your own life, you're then able to care for others and see their needs and desires in a new way. You can't pour from an empty dipper, and self-care allows you the space and clarity to do what you can to send compassion out into the world.

Starting a Self-Care Routine

Self-care should be treated as a ritual in your life, something you make the time to pause for, no matter what. You are important. You deserve rejuvenation and a sense of relaxation. You need to open your soul to the gifts that the universe is giving you, and self-care provides you with a way to ensure you're ready to receive those gifts. To begin a self-care routine, start by making yourself the priority. Do the customized rituals in Part 2 with intention, knowing the universe has already given them to you, by virtue of your sign and your governing element.

Now that you understand the role that self-care will hold in your life, let's take a closer look at the connection between self-care and astrology.

CHAPTER 2

SELF-CARE AND ASTROLOGY

✳

Astrology is the study of the connection between the objects in the heavens (the planets, the stars) and what happens here on earth. Just as the movements of the planets and other heavenly bodies influence the ebb and flow of the tides, so do they influence you—your body, your mind, your spirit. This relationship is ever present and is never more important—or personal—than when viewed through the lens of self-care.

In this chapter you'll learn how the locations of these celestial bodies at the time of your birth affect you and define the self-care activities that will speak directly to you as a Leo, an Aries, a Capricorn, or any of the other zodiac signs. You'll see how the zodiac influences every part of your being and why ignoring its lessons can leave you feeling frustrated and unfulfilled. You'll also realize that, when you perform the rituals of self-care based on your sign, the wisdom of the cosmos will lead you down a path of fulfillment and restoration—to the return of who you really are, deep inside.

Zodiac Polarities

In astrology, all signs are mirrored by other signs that are on the opposite side of the zodiac. This polarity ensures that the zodiac is balanced and continues to flow with an unbreakable, even stream of energy. There are two different polarities in the zodiac and each is called by a number of different names:

* Yang/masculine/positive polarity
* Yin/feminine/negative polarity

Each polar opposite embodies a number of opposing traits, qualities, and attributes that will influence which self-care practices will work for or against your sign and your own personal sense of cosmic balance.

Yang

Whether male or female, those who fall under yang, or masculine, signs are extroverted and radiate their energy outward. They are spontaneous, active, bold, and fearless. They move forward in life with the desire to enjoy everything the world has to offer to them, and they work hard to transfer their inspiration and positivity to others so that those individuals may experience the same gifts that the universe offers them. All signs governed by the fire and air elements are yang and hold the potential for these dominant qualities. We will refer to them with masculine pronouns. These signs are:

* Aries
* Leo
* Sagittarius
* Gemini
* Libra
* Aquarius

There are people who hold yang energy who are introverted and retiring. However, by practicing self-care that is customized for your sign and understanding the potential ways to use your energy, you can find a way—perhaps one that's unique to you—to claim your native buoyancy and dominance and engage with the path that the universe opens for you.

Yin

Whether male or female, those who fall under yin, or feminine, signs are introverted and radiate inwardly. They draw people and experiences to them rather than seeking people and experiences in an extroverted way. They move forward in life with an energy that is reflective, receptive, and focused on communication and achieving shared goals. All signs governed by the earth and water elements are yin and hold the potential for these reflective qualities. We will refer to them with feminine pronouns. These signs are:

* Taurus
* Virgo
* Capricorn
* Cancer
* Scorpio
* Pisces

As there are people with yang energy who are introverted and retiring, there are also people with yin energy who are outgoing and extroverted. And by practicing self-care rituals that speak to your particular sign, energy, and governing body, you will reveal your true self and the balance of energy will be maintained.

Governing Elements

Each astrological sign has a governing element that defines their energy orientation and influences both the way the sign moves through the universe and relates to self-care. The elements are fire, earth, air, and water. All the signs in each element share certain characteristics, along with having their own sign-specific qualities:

* **Fire:** Fire signs are adventurous, bold, and energetic. They enjoy the heat and warm environments and look to the sun and fire as a means to recharge their depleted batteries. They're competitive, outgoing, and passionate. The fire signs are Aries, Leo, and Sagittarius.
* **Earth:** Earth signs all share a common love and tendency toward a practical, material, sensual, and economic orientation. The earth signs are Taurus, Virgo, and Capricorn.
* **Air:** Air is the most ephemeral element and those born under this element are thinkers, innovators, and communicators. The air signs are Gemini, Libra, and Aquarius.
* **Water:** Water signs are instinctual, compassionate, sensitive, and emotional. The water signs are Cancer, Scorpio, and Pisces.

Chapter 3 teaches you all about the ways your specific governing element influences and drives your connection to your cosmically harmonious self-care rituals, but it's important that you realize how important these elemental traits are to your self-care practice and to the activities that will help restore and reveal your true self.

Sign Qualities

Each of the astrological elements governs three signs. Each of these three signs is also given its own quality or mode, which corresponds to a different part of each season: the beginning, the middle, or the end.

* **Cardinal signs:** The cardinal signs initiate and lead in each season. Like something that is just starting out, they are actionable, enterprising, and assertive, and are born leaders. The cardinal signs are Aries, Cancer, Libra, and Capricorn.
* **Fixed signs:** The fixed signs come into play when the season is well established. They are definite, consistent, reliable, motivated by principles, and powerfully stubborn. The fixed signs are Taurus, Leo, Scorpio, and Aquarius.
* **Mutable signs:** The mutable signs come to the forefront when the seasons are changing. They are part of one season, but also part of the next. They are adaptable, versatile, and flexible. The mutable signs are Gemini, Virgo, Sagittarius, and Pisces.

Each of these qualities tells you a lot about yourself and who you are. They also give you invaluable information about the types of self-care rituals that your sign will find the most intuitive and helpful.

Ruling Planets

In addition to qualities and elements, each specific sign is ruled by a particular planet that lends its personality to those born under that sign. Again, these sign-specific traits give you valuable insight into the personality of the signs and the self-care rituals that may best rejuvenate them. The signs that correspond to each planet—and the ways that those planetary influences determine your self-care options—are as follows:

* **Aries:** Ruled by Mars, Aries is passionate, energetic, and determined.
* **Taurus:** Ruled by Venus, Taurus is sensual, romantic, and fertile.
* **Gemini:** Ruled by Mercury, Gemini is intellectual, changeable, and talkative.
* **Cancer:** Ruled by the Moon, Cancer is nostalgic, emotional, and home loving.
* **Leo:** Ruled by the Sun, Leo is fiery, dramatic, and confident.
* **Virgo:** Ruled by Mercury, Virgo is intellectual, analytical, and responsive.
* **Libra:** Ruled by Venus, Libra is beautiful, romantic, and graceful.
* **Scorpio:** Ruled by Mars and Pluto, Scorpio is intense, powerful, and magnetic.
* **Sagittarius:** Ruled by Jupiter, Sagittarius is optimistic, boundless, and larger than life.

* **Capricorn:** Ruled by Saturn, Capricorn is wise, patient, and disciplined.
* **Aquarius:** Ruled by Uranus, Aquarius is independent, unique, and eccentric.
* **Pisces:** Ruled by Neptune and Jupiter, Pisces is dreamy, sympathetic, and idealistic.

A Word on Sun Signs

When someone is a Leo, Aries, Sagittarius, or any of the other zodiac signs, it means that the sun was positioned in this constellation in the heavens when they were born. Your Sun sign is a dominant factor in defining your personality, your best self-care practices, and your soul nature. Every person also has the position of the Moon, Mercury, Venus, Mars, Jupiter, Saturn, Uranus, Neptune, and Pluto. These planets can be in any of the elements: fire signs, earth signs, air signs, or water signs. If you have your entire chart calculated by an astrologer or on an Internet site, you can see the whole picture and learn about all your elements. Someone born under Leo with many signs in another element will not be as concentrated in the fire element as someone with five or six planets in Leo. Someone born in Pisces with many signs in another element will not be as concentrated in the water element as someone with five or six planets in Pisces. And so on. Astrology is a complex system and has many shades of meaning. For our purposes looking at the self-care practices designated by your Sun sign, or what most people consider their sign, will give you the information you need to move forward and find fulfillment and restoration.

CHAPTER 3

ESSENTIAL ELEMENTS:
EARTH

✳

The earth element is most familiar to all of us, for the earth is our home. We are born on this planet and are the custodians of her beauty, natural resources, health, and well-being. There is an intimate connection between human beings and the balance of the earth's conditions. The earth signs (Taurus, Virgo, and Capricorn) feel this connection more than other signs, and their approach to self-care reflects their relationship with this natural element. They are practical and realistic, and they need self-care techniques that match their disposition. More so, earth signs are rooted in the material, physical world. They are, at their best, pragmatic, sensual, patient, and grounded. At their worst they can be greedy, lascivious, and materialistic.

Most humans face the polarity of balancing the need and competition of making a living, with the dreams and desires of their heart. Earth signs accept this as reality instead of fighting against it. Becoming successful in the material world is their natural inclination. Any self-care they do must reflect that ultimate goal as well. Let's take a look at the mythological importance of the earth and its counterparts, the basic characteristics of the three earth signs, and what they all have in common when it comes to self-care.

The Mythology of Earth

There are many creation myths from all over the world. Most of these myths feature a Mother Earth figure. In Greek mythology, which forms the basis for much of astrology, Gaia was the Earth Mother. She represented the circle of life. Gaia came out of chaos and gave birth to Ouranos, the sky god, who also happened to be her husband. (The Greeks liked to keep things in the family.) The relationship between Gaia and Ouranos was so passionate that their children could not emerge from Gaia's womb. One of these unborn children was Cronos who in Roman astrology was called Saturn. Cronos decided to overthrow Ouranos and in the womb emasculated his father. And the sky separated from the earth. Cronos, the lord of time, ruled the universe for a time but later got his comeuppance as Zeus/Jupiter displaced him and became the chief god and ruler of all. These myths regarding the separation of earth and sky (or heaven and earth) abound in ancient world cultures.

Earth signs strive for measured success, and often seek worldly possessions to solidify their self-worth. This need for stability is indicative of their element. Earth, after all, is the foundation for life. It is tangible, solid, and defined. Many earth signs are so grounded in reality they can lose track of their emotional well-being. Self-care rituals that cater to both mind and soul are key for earth signs. Simplicity and practicality are often paramount.

The Element of Earth

Earth signs are known for their measured approach to life. They are typically patient, reliable, and disciplined, traits that often lead to prosperity. Because of this, earth signs are often viewed as well balanced and levelheaded, hence the saying *down-to-earth*. Earth signs are known as the sensible, pragmatic signs, choosing to focus on practical solutions over emotions. They are not light and buoyant like air signs, passionate and fiery like fire signs, nor empathetic and fluid like water signs. Instead, they are committed, strong, and trustworthy. For example, Taurus is loyal and always ready to help friends and family in need. Virgo is hardworking and will never back down from a challenge. And Capricorn is responsible and will help others stick to their responsibilities as well.

Astrological Symbols

The astrological symbols (also called the zodiacal symbols) of the earth signs also give you hints as to how earth signs move through the world. Each symbol ties back to the nature associated with earth signs:

* Taurus is the Bull
* Virgo is the Maiden gathering the harvest
* Capricorn is the Goat

All these signs show steadfast and intimate harmony with the cycles of the seasons and a personal connection with the earth: the meadows, green fields, and rocks. Taurus comes from ancient myths about the cults that worshipped the bull as a fertility symbol. She represents coiled power not yet unleashed. Virgo is the only earth sign that has a human symbol. She is a mutable sign and like a junior Mother Earth. Capricorn is of the earth but climbs the mountains of ambition and spiritual ascent. Each earth sign's personality and subsequent approach to self-care connect to the qualities of these representative symbols.

Signs and Seasonal Modes

Each of the elements in astrology also has a sign that corresponds to a different part of each season.

* **Fixed:** Taurus, the first earth sign, comes when spring is in full bloom. Taurus is called a fixed earth sign because she comes when the season is well established. The fixed signs are definite, motivated by principles, and powerfully stubborn.
* **Mutable:** Virgo, the second earth sign, moves us from summer to autumn. These signs are called mutable. In terms of character the mutable signs are changeable and flexible.
* **Cardinal:** Capricorn is the leader of the earth signs because she marks the beginning of winter and the time around the winter solstice.

If you know your element and whether you are a cardinal, fixed, or mutable sign, you know a lot about yourself. This is invaluable for self-care and is reflected in the customized earth sign self-care rituals found in Part 2.

Earth Signs and Self-Care

The earth signs' first motivation in life is to feel comfortable in their physical surroundings. For physical self-care their most important motivation is routine and diligence. Earth signs don't require a lot of variety. Their motto is, "If something works, keep it." The downside to this attitude is that earth signs can get stuck in a rut, but the benefits of continuous physical exercise, self-care, and good diet at all ages are the cornerstones of comfort for earth signs.

You may notice that earth signs touch other people more frequently than other elements do. They pat, reach out, hug, and extend themselves physically to others. They also have an intimate and close sense of personal space and will be up-front and personal in encountering new people or old friends. They want and need to sense the whole person.

Earth signs take self-care actions in a very practical way. For example, if an earth sign wants to exercise more, they may think the following: "If I can exercise more, I will lose weight and be healthier, so I will have more years to build my business, enjoy my family, and do what I want."

Spiritually, earth signs feel little division between body and soul. If they feel comfortable and well physically, then their soul qualities can evolve and blossom. Some people may feel that the high-minded notion of spiritual retreat and meditation defines a spiritual person, and they therefore look down on an earth sign's practical thoughts, such as "How much will it cost to go on this retreat and how much time will it take?" Earth signs don't consider this to be materialism at the expense of spirituality. Instead, to them, it is a clear recognition of the practical and sensible way the world works. Ashrams, well-being programs, herbs, and health practices cost money, and it is a reasonable question to ask if the practice is worth it.

The most important "rule" for earth signs is that self-care feed the senses. Whatever the plan is, it should include every sense. The activity must look appealing, smell good, taste good, sound good, and feel good. The more all the senses are involved, the happier the earth signs will be and the more likely they will be to follow the program. If the price is reasonable, so much the better. But too much sensual input can cause earth signs to overindulge and become lethargic. This is a potential pitfall for all the earth signs.

The overall purpose and meaning of the earth signs is to offer practical solutions to maintain personal self-care and the health of the planet. The earth signs have a lot to teach the people around them. Modern life is increasingly jagged. The earth signs demonstrate the value of solid measured progress. Walk don't run, and take things as they come. This attitude can preserve each of us as well as planet earth.

So now that you know what earth signs need to practice self-care, let's look at the devoted characteristics of Taurus and how she can maintain her inner balance.

CHAPTER 4

SELF-CARE FOR TAURUS

✳

Dates: April 20–May 20
Element: Earth
Polarity: Yin
Quality: Fixed
Symbol: Bull
Ruler: Venus

Taurus is the first earth sign of the zodiac. She is a fixed sign, which means that her season, spring, is in full bloom and well established. The fixed signs are also known as the "serpent signs" of the zodiac. In the Hindu tradition the serpent power is called kundalini energy ("the juice of life"), and it travels from the root chakra at the base of the spine to the crown chakra at the top of the head. As the first fixed or "serpent" sign, Taurus has this kundalini energy in abundance, but it is not yet fully expressed; it lies latent.

Though she is a powerful and determined force when she sets her mind to something, she cannot be pushed or forced to do what she is not inclined to do. Taurus takes time to adjust to new ideas and situations. Though it is rare, her power can erupt into anger, and much like her symbol, the Bull, she will see red. Patience is key when Taurus is in this mood; it is best to wait until things calm down on their own: the mood will pass.

The Taurus glyph (picture) represents the head and horns of a bull. The bull is a symbol of rich, fertile power. In ancient Greece the beginning of Taurus was celebrated as the feast of Maia (similar to the traditional May Day), with the sun represented by a white bull with a golden disc hanging between its horns, followed by a procession of virgins who exemplified the fertility of nature in the spring.

A Greek myth to consider for Taurus is that of Europa and Zeus. Europa, a beautiful Phoenician princess and mortal, had a dream that two continents were trying to possess her. The first, Asia, was where she was born and where she lived with her family; the other continent was nameless. Awakening, she went out to gather flowers. Looking down from Olympus, the god Zeus desired Europa, and to escape the watchful and jealous eye of his wife, Hera, he turned himself into a beautiful bull, spiriting Europa away to the island of Crete. Zeus went on to other lovers, but Europa remained in Crete and gave birth to three sons. Europe, the other continent Europa had dreamed about, eventually was named after her. This ancient story speaks to Taurus's love of land and nature, as well as her connection to the bull.

Self-Care and Taurus

Taurus's ruler is Venus, the planet of romance, pleasure, and beauty. Taurus loves the way beauty feels. She likes to touch materials, people, trees—anything. The texture of what she touches communicates directly to her senses and impacts how she perceives the material world around her. Taurus's sensuality also extends to food and drink.

The tantalizing powers of Venus can also incline people to be overindulgent, and in terms of self-care this is where Taurus will need to be mindful. Appreciating the tastes of food and drink, and the feel of bodily pleasure is good, but if this appreciation becomes unbalanced, there is a tendency to fall into a case of the "too much" syndrome (too much food, too much drink, too much relaxation), which can lead to a decline in energy and mood. If Taurus falls into this rut, it can be hard to break out of, because no matter what Taurus is doing, she likes routine. And if the routine is pleasurable, Taurus will need to tap into her strong bovine willpower to break the cycle.

Taurus Rules the Neck, Ears, and Cerebellum

Taurus rules over the neck, cerebellum, and ears, so self-care related to these parts of the body is especially important. Like her celestial symbol, the Bull, the defining features of Taurus are a thick neck and small ears. Shoulder and neck rolls should be a part of her daily exercise, as tension can often form in these areas. Using yoga foam rolls to massage the spine and neck area will prevent soreness and help move energy through the body.

Perhaps more important than the outer neck muscles, however, is the throat. Taurus is connected to the throat chakra, which controls expression of thought and emotion. Taurus should consider wearing a scarf in both the cold and warm months to protect against cold drafts and sunburn, so her voice is always loud and clear. The throat is also key in singing and humming, activities which come naturally to Taurus. Many great singers, pop and opera alike, are Taurean. Bing Crosby may be from a past time, but his rich, crooning style is a hallmark of Taurus's sensual approach to life. Singing in the shower is a primo self-care activity. There should be no room for judgment: just letting her voice resonate in those great shower acoustics is a perfect activity for Taurus! And while doing chores, humming is a great way to keep stress levels low. Taurus should also consider singing herself a lullaby before she falls asleep. The soft music will prepare both her mind and body for dreamland.

Just as essential as outward expression is the Taurus ability to listen and reflect inwardly with the information she collects. To keep her ears alert and healthy, she should be mindful of temperature changes and wear earmuffs or warm hats in colder weather. She should also avoid prolonged periods of loud noise that could damage her hearing.

Taurus also rules the cerebellum, which controls movement, coordination, and balance. Exercises that improve and build on good motor function and rhythm are important to the Taurean wellness. Great sports for coordination and motor function include tennis and combat routines. Taurus also has a flair for contact sports that require muscular endurance, such as boxing, and many champion fighters have been Taurus. Coupling exercise with music through dance is the best way for Taurus to keep her rhythm and enjoy exercising. Once Taurus finds a routine that works, she will keep it. If part of Taurus's routine involves extended periods of joint pressure, such as running on a treadmill, it can cause stress on the body because of the repetitive pounding. Taurus's great asset is continuity and routine, but if this routine locks in tense muscle patterns, it becomes counterproductive.

Taurus and Self-Care Success

The first step in good self-care for Taurus is feeding the senses moderately. Taurus is especially susceptible to every sound, taste, touch, or smell, and this can easily lead to a sense overload that leaves her overwhelmed and unmotivated to do anything—except run from it all. She will be led to successful self-care by the promise of feeling better and the pride in mastering self-control.

If part of Taurus's self-care involves meeting with a personal counselor or other wellness adviser, she must have an emotional bond with that person. Again, Taurus's senses are heightened, so she needs an established connection and foundation of trust to properly interpret and absorb what that person is expressing. A pitfall in counseling for Taurus lies in her resistance to change. If she feels she is being ordered or pushed toward something new, she can become stubborn, either closing herself off to the idea, or doing the exact opposite. Guiding her toward improved self-care in a more indirect way will lead to a successful change.

A key sense that is highly developed in Taurus is the sense of smell, which can be instrumental in her self-care. Many "noses" who work in the perfume industry are Taureans. They can detect notes of different oils and essences, and blend them to create a wonderful perfume. Even if you are not a professional "nose," the power of scent can relax or invigorate, improve mood, recall happy memories, promote communication, and change the entire atmosphere of a space. Taurus should implement different scents into her self-care routine. For example, if she was a bit indulgent the night before, a whiff of diluted (according to instructions) peppermint or bergamot essential oil will encourage her to practice more self-control the following day.

As in counseling, pitfalls to successful self-care for Taurus are overly disciplined approaches to anything. Taurus needs to feel relaxed about any kind of program.

She wants the good feelings of exercising her body, and the pleasure of knowing that her body and mind are in control. A sure-fire way for Taurus to stick to a self-care routine is to "pay" herself for every good action she takes toward caring for herself. This can be in the form of a treat such as a new scarf or eating dinner out, or as a certain amount of money that she moves into a savings account. For all of Taurus's appreciation for the finer things, she understands the importance of spending her money wisely and a boost to her savings will be just the motivation she needs to reach her goals.

In terms of her soul development, Taurus shares an intimate relationship with both spirituality and the physical world. She views the two as entwined, each growing and balancing the other. Spirituality also goes hand in hand with generosity and kindness for Taurus, and as a nature lover, this kindness extends to the earth. Restorative self-care practices for Taurus will allow her to balance her spirituality with her love for the natural world. Strong and patient just like her element, earth, Taurus values stability and determination. What she shows is that steady progress can bring about actions that make a difference in both personal well-being and the well-being of the world around her.

Be they physical or mental, self-care practices are vital to a healthy, happy Bull. So let's take a look at the self-care activities tailored specifically to you, Taurus.

PART 2

SELF-CARE
RITUALS
— FOR —
TAURUS

Break Free from Your Comfort Zone

As an earth sign, you tend to be organized, ritualistic, and highly structured. However, because you like structure and rituals so much, you can easily fall into repeating patterns, and even if that pattern is not particularly healthy, you'll stay with it. Once you're in a comfortable place, it's hard for you to change your habits. But being afraid to change something can hold you back from making life-changing decisions or improving yourself. Getting out of your regular rituals will boost your confidence and open up new doors in your life. Make a choice to break out of your routine and try something new.

Get Stepping

In terms of fitness, earth signs like measurable results. They like to be able to calculate situations and use concrete facts to do so. This is why a pedometer, smart watch, or fitness tracker would be perfect for you. You like to be able to know the exact number of steps you have taken so you can use that information to plan, to calculate further exercise or meals, or as a motivator for yourself. Those folks who go willy-nilly into exercise are not for you; hard facts and organization will get the job done for an earth sign.

Don a Cashmere Scarf

Taurus rules the neck and throat. It is important for her to keep her throat chakra open as it promotes self-expression and communication with others. Tying a yellow scarf around your neck will encourage the sharing of your ideas, as well as restore energy to turn those creative thoughts into actions. A light blue scarf will promote communication and a sense of stability when you may be feeling less steady on your feet in your social or private life. Try cashmere, as it is a stimulating textile for the luxury loving Bull.

Promote Abundance with Emeralds

Invoking the feelings of nature, rich-in-color emeralds welcome abundance and confidence into your life. Wear an emerald in a ring or bracelet where you can always see it to feel more grounded.

This deep green gem also has a calming effect on emotions. Ruled by Venus, Taurus often has numerous feelings coursing through her at all times. She is especially sensitive to the actions of those around her, and these interactions can drive her mood. Wearing an emerald (or two or three) can help keep your emotions in check.

Do Some Heavy Lifting

Earth signs are incredibly strong people, mentally and physically. With that in mind, make sure you emphasize weight and strength training in your workouts. Develop your lifting muscles by exercising with weights and concentrating on weight-bearing exercises throughout your life. There are so many variations of weight and strength training that you can easily find a routine that suits your age, strength, general health, and energy level. Strength training will help you fight the loss of muscle, bone mass, and strength that occurs naturally with aging. It is also great for your joints, an area of concern for a lot of earth signs.

Heal Your Spirit with a Garden

You are an earth sign, after all. What could be more in tune with your nature than to work with the earth? As an earth sign, you tend to hold on to stress and have trouble releasing it, but working with the soil will bring you into a state of calmness. When you are connected to an element, just being near it and working with it can help realign your energy and bring peace.

So go out and till your soil, buy seeds or plants, and then plant them in precise and organized rows. As you watch your plants grow and tend to them, you will discover your stress will wash away. Even if you don't have space to plant a garden where you live, just getting your hands in the soil will help heal your spirit.

Protect Your Ears

The perceptive Taurus's ears are very sensitive to noise and temperature. Promote the health of your ears with proper protection from the elements. Wear earmuffs or a hat in cold weather, and keep the volume at a moderate level when using headphones. If you notice a frequent ringing sensation in your ears, make an appointment with your doctor to check for causes and treatment. Taurus is a master of listening and reflection—so keep your ears protected and on alert!

Give Yourself Some Time

E arth signs are grounded, logical, and reliable, so it goes without saying that you hate to be late. In fact, punctuality is an admired quality of the earth signs. If a situation occurs that causes you to be late, it can fill you with stress and cause anxiety. So, with that in mind, make a point of giving yourself some extra time to get where you need to be. This will give a cushion in case some unexpected events pop up and delay you. You know being late will stress you out, so do your mind and spirit a favor and try to eliminate anything that might interfere with your timeliness.

Encourage Openness
with Ylang-Ylang

Taurus is a sign of reflection and deep, intrapersonal thought—but it is just as important to have an open flow of communication with others. An ingredient found in many perfumes, ylang-ylang promotes social connections and a feeling of intimacy in your relationships. You can very sparingly dab the essential oil (diluted according to instructions) on your neck, or diffuse it in a communal space such as the living room or an open work area. It also boosts overall mood and energy levels (which is helpful when there are things to do, but your bed is calling your name).

Collect Dolls

———————————

Taurus is a collector. Ruled by Venus, she is a sentimental sign who loves keepsakes. She will enjoy collecting dolls, which can hold memories of her childhood, and can also appreciate in value over time. Antique dolls are also a good choice, as Taurus will admire the beauty and tradition of the dolls, as well as the craftsmanship used in earlier times. She may also consider eventually passing on the dolls to a younger loved one, who will cherish the dolls and carry on their tradition.

Take a Woodworking Class

Taurus loves working with her hands, feeling the sensation of tools in her hands as she gets to work. She also loves the sense of accomplishment in creating something useful! Tap into both sensation and utility with a woodworking class. An instructor will show you how to safely use the different tools to shape the wood, and you get to return home with your masterpiece and a sense of accomplishment—plus some wood shavings everywhere. Fortunately, earthy Taurus doesn't mind.

Keep Things Slow and Steady

Earth signs know that nothing great ever comes easily or quickly. In fact, their combined patience and discipline is one of their most admirable traits and allows them to stick things out for the long run. Earth signs like to meticulously plan and *hate* to rush. Actually, rushing through a task will cause you stress and may lead to mistakes (something you don't tolerate well). Whether working or playing, you should take a slow and steady approach, and your final results will be better quality and more long-lasting than those of the hurried competition. Keep a steady pace when at home and at work and you'll produce your best results.

Open Up to Love
with Rose Quartz

Pink and sweet, rose quartz is the stone of Taurus's planetary ruler, Venus. The celestial embodiment of love, Venus influences the emotions of Taurus. A stone of love itself, rose quartz opens you up to love of all kinds, and helps you to understand the perspective of a romantic partner, close friend, or family member, strengthening your connection. A smooth piece of rose quartz held in your left hand or kept in your left pocket will keep your communication centers open and your emotions calm.

Learn at Your Own Pace

As an earth sign, you love to learn new things and are not dissuaded when the subject seems difficult or arduous. Persistence is definitely an earth sign characteristic! But while you love to discover new skills, you don't like being monitored while you do so. You learn better while working solo and do not like to have someone looking over your shoulder. Often methodical and meticulous, you have no patience for those who want to just jump in and go with it. So don't put yourself through that! If you are part of a group for work or school, try suggesting that everyone work on ideas separately and then reconvene to discuss them. That way you can have your solo learning time while still being a team player!

Eat What You Love

Earth signs love their foods, and they especially like to be relaxed and savor their food when they eat it. However, many earth signs have sensitive palates and have to be choosey about what they eat. You need to listen to your body about what it needs and what it can tolerate, and when you find a food you like, enjoy it! Also, being conscious about what foods you are putting in your body is important for earth signs. When you can, try to choose foods grown without pesticides, added hormones, or artificial fertilizers as many of these things can irritate your body. Go with natural and organic versions of the foods you love.

Build Endurance
with Your Workouts

E xercise is proven to be one of the best forms of
self-care you can do for your body and mind. But
what if you are new to working out or just feel like it
isn't your thing? Fortunately for you as an earth sign,
the slow and steady approach also relates to how you
should be working out. Earth signs are disciplined,
dependable, and committed. So, when they exercise,
they should choose workouts that require patience,
precision, and a set routine.

Workouts that work your muscles at a slower pace
will build your endurance and muscle strength without
making you feel like your regime is hectic and out of
your control. Training for races that require precision
and problem-solving like a Tough Mudder, which is
more about endurance than speed, is also a hit with
earth signs.

Relax with Vanilla Oil

Rich, and containing a touch of sweetness, vanilla oil boosts mood, helps you to unwind after a long day, and also contains a number of other healing properties such as antioxidants, anti-inflammatories, and antibacterials. Comfort-loving Taurus need not hear any more. You can dab the oil (diluted according to instructions) behind your ears, or diffuse it in a calm setting, such as your bedroom or beside your bathtub.

Indulge in the Warmth of Cinnamon

Nothing conjures up feelings of warmth like the smell of cinnamon. It brings back memories of warm, comforting foods on cool, crisp fall days. But cinnamon is not just for autumn time; in fact, it is perfect for earth signs to use all year round. When you're cooking, choose warm spices like cinnamon over sharp and peppery spices, as these tend not to agree with an earth sign's delicate palate. As an added bonus, cinnamon is good for your heart health, helps regulate your blood sugar, boosts your brain function, and offers your body protection from diabetes.

Cinnamon is a marvelous addition to both sweet and savory meals and will add the hint of spice you crave without the burning aftereffects of other spices. Add cinnamon to your favorite foods including oatmeal, pancakes, yogurt, peanut or almond butter, chilies and soups, and even your coffee!

Try a Dessert Wine

Entertaining guests or looking for a sweet host gift? Purchase a dessert wine, or a selection of dessert wines, to have on hand. Ruled by sensual Venus, Taurus loves tantalizing flavors that ignite her sensitive taste buds. And sharing a luxurious treat with her friends or family is the icing on the cake!

Rich and sweet, dessert wines are made by adding in sugar or reducing the amount of water used in the fermentation process. In some cases, the grapes are even dried first to make a raisin wine. As a rule of thumb, the wine should be sweeter than the food it is paired with. It makes a wonderful companion to fresh fruits, custard, or semisweet biscuits.

Embrace the Possibilities

Nod your head frequently to give a positive yes to the day—and also to keep the neck area relaxed and flexible. Taurus knows the importance of stability, but change is just as crucial to personal growth. Say yes to what comes your way! You can also massage your muscles as you nod. One simple technique is pushing your fingers from your shoulders in toward your neck, then lightly pushing down on the muscle connecting your neck and shoulders.

Avoid Neck Pain
with Lateral Raises

—————

Weighted lateral raises are a great way to strengthen Taurus's thick muscles and avoid tension buildup in the neck due to inactivity. They can also ease any neck strain you may currently have. Be careful of training your neck muscles with intense or improper lifting practices.

To do the lateral raise, stand straight with your feet shoulder-width apart and your knees slightly bent. If you are a beginner, you should start with one 4–9 pound weight (based on your individual weight and fitness; ask your fitness trainer for weight and technique guidance) in each hand. Lift your arms up straight at your sides until they are parallel with the floor. Slowly lower your arms, then repeat eight to twelve times per set.

Slip Into a Turtleneck

———————

S tylish and cozy, a turtleneck is the perfect addition to the Taurean closet. The unique design of the turtleneck protects the throat and neck, which are ruled by Taurus. It is important for Taurus to be mindful of these areas, which are vital to her self-expression and can be sensitive to cold weather and direct sunlight. Keep a collection of turtlenecks in different Taurean colors, such as green and pink. Be sure to invest in soft fabrics that will soothe your throat and remind you to be gentle with yourself.

Take a Mud Bath

Who knew dirt could be so good for you? Not only is a mud bath soothing and great for your skin—but it can also magnetize your earthy celestial side. Treat yourself to a trip to a spa mud bath. The mud is the perfect cooling element for earth-bound Taurus, and her heightened Venusian senses will delight in the tactile experience. If you have any pesky blemishes, a mud bath will also help release the built-up oils and dirt from your pores. You can find mud bath options at many spa locations. Take some time for yourself and recline in earthy luxury.

Treat Yourself to Chocolate

E arth signs love chocolate, and it's a wonderful way to treat yourself. Some earth signs may have trouble with dairy though, so try a good-quality rich dark chocolate to indulge in. Not only does dark chocolate taste heavenly, but it benefits your health too. Dark chocolate helps lower blood pressure, is a powerful source of antioxidants, and reduces your heart disease risk. Eat your dark chocolate straight—or melt some in a double boiler, pour into a silicone mold ice cube tray, sprinkle on some healthy nuts and dried fruits, and allow to set for a mouthwatering treat you can feel good about.

Stick with the Classics

Treat yourself to a little shopping trip, but rather than buying the latest fad, shop for your sign. Style magazines and experts may tell you what's all the rage in fashion, but as an earth sign, you won't necessarily feel comfortable or strong—both things earth signs need in their lives—with what is trendy. Earth signs are all about the simple yet elegant look when it comes to fashion, as well as décor. You like things that are classic, well made, neat, and polished—think Audrey Hepburn (who is also an earth sign!) and George Clooney.

In terms of clothing, you feel more comfortable in the elegant and sophisticated and stay clear of the flashy, too tight, or too revealing. You value comfort, but that doesn't mean you don't look suave or glamorous; you like to make a statement without seeming like you are making a statement. So stick with the classics and you'll always exude an understated elegance.

Adopt a Bull (Dog)

An ideal pet for Taurus is the English bulldog. Just like Taurus, bulldogs are strong, loyal, and fond of a lot of relaxation. Owning a dog will also establish a routine of walking and feeding times—stability that Taurus will enjoy bringing into her life.

Not ready to adopt? You can spend quality time with a bulldog through volunteering at a rescue, or by downloading an app that connects pet owners to local people like you who can take their dog for a walk when they get stuck late at the office or are away for a short time.

Protect Your Throat

Earth signs are connected to several parts of the body including the throat. Communication is key to earth signs, and when something interferes with that communication, whether it be a blocked throat chakra or even a sore throat, earth signs' confidence and strength can suffer. So protect your throat! In the colder months wear a scarf or muffler around your throat. Try meditating with turquoise to open up your throat chakra. If you do get a sore throat, treat it quickly and naturally with a saltwater gargle, honey, lemon water, or ginger tea.

Reach for Your Goals

Once earth signs know what they want, they will stay the course until they get it. Earth signs are strong and disciplined people, so use that tenacity to achieve the things you want most in life. Use your detail-oriented, driven brain and create a goal board. List the things you most want to accomplish and post them up where you can see them every day. This way you can be sure to keep your goals fresh in your mind and on the top of your to-do list. Also make sure the goals you write on your board are clear and actionable. Whatever your goal is, this visual reminder is key to helping you stay focused and on track.

Try Acupuncture

Every Taurus knows the healing power of touch, especially as a great way to relieve and release tension in the body. As an earth sign and headstrong Bull, Taurus can often hold on to certain things—physical or emotional—and this weight places stress on her body.

Acupuncture is a wonderful way to pull this stress out of your joints and muscles. As you relax, an acupuncturist uses different pressure points on your body to balance your energy, diminishing headaches, joint pain, muscle soreness, menstrual discomfort, and more!

Create a Room of Comfort

Everyone needs a space, even if it is just one room in your house or apartment, where you can just get away and relax in comfort. Comfortable surroundings are important for earth signs in particular; not only do they crave them, but they also feel the most at peace there.

So make sure at least one room in your home is filled with plush, cushy furniture. Big pieces of furniture are important for comfort, too, because they give you a sense of security and a feeling that you are staying put. Overstuffed pillows and soft blankets would make nice accents here as well. Create a room that makes you feel safe and snug, a place you can go to find relaxation and peace and forget the stresses of your life, and you will be a truly happy earth sign.

Accent Your Home
with Lily of the Valley

Taurus has a keen sense of smell, and the aromas she surrounds herself with play an important role in her mood and her perception of the world around her. Lily of the valley is a simple yet elegant flower that features a sweet, classic floral scent.

Place attractive vases of lily of the valley around your home to evoke the refreshing aura of spring and nature's gorgeous springtime bounty. The flower's scent can draw any points of stress out of the room, opening up the space for your creativity and powerful Taurean spirit to flourish.

Slip Into Pastels

—————————

Pastel colors suit Taurus, as they are reminiscent of spring and all of its natural abundance. Muted yellow, peach, light blue, and pink hues grace her flourishing birth season. If the weather has been unfavorable, or you are feeling stuck in a place of discouragement, slip into a soft pastel shirt or dress. You'll magnetize the invigorating and inspirational essence of spring—and give yourself some much-needed pampering to boot.

For an extra touch of spring, no matter the weather, you can paint a wall or room in your home with a pastel shade. Light blue walls in your bedroom promote relaxation and restful sleep, while a yellow living or home office space boosts creativity.

Wrap Yourself in Warmth

There is something so special and nurturing about being wrapped in something cuddly. Earth signs especially like to feel warm, protected, and comfortable. A good way to accomplish this feeling in your home is to find a thick, warm comforter for your bed. Bonus points if you can make one yourself, maybe even stitching in some pieces of a childhood blankie. Not a crafty person? There is no shortage of ultra-plush comforters available to buy online. Try to get one in a deep, rich earth tone to compliment your earth sign! Want to kick the comfort up a notch? Try warming your sheets in the dryer right before you get into bed!

Make Your Home Your Haven

Earth signs like to feel protected in their home, almost as if it were a sheltered cave. A feeling of enclosure may seem stifling to other signs, but for earth signs there is a comfort in the closeness and warmth. Emphasize that feeling in your home by decorating with darker colors and with accents such as lamps with shades to give off a soft glow in your rooms. This warm and welcoming shelter will make you feel protected and safe whenever you enter it.

Drum It Out

Though Taurus is usually temperate, sometimes the sparks fly and she needs to blow off a bit of steam. Purchase a small drum to take out when you need to release frustration or stress. The vibrating rhythm of the drumming, as well as the sounds, will ease you of negative energy while tapping into your love of music. Taurus enjoys using her hands, so the best drums for her are the conga, bongo, or other traditional hand drums. For a bit of extra flair, a tambourine allows you to drum *and* shake things out.

Color Your Home
Like the Earth

Earth signs tend to feel most at ease in their homes when they are surrounded by calming earth tones. Greens, browns, and whites are great choices to decorate your home. Of course, given your simple tastes, you'll want to make sure these colors are muted versions, nothing too garish or bright. Loud colors will actually take away from your comfort level at home, something you don't want to do. Also wood floors, dark finishes, and plain walls will all add to the elegance and polished feeling of your home while fitting in perfectly with your classic and understated vibe.

Indulge in Rich Flavors

Rich, unique flavors, coffee and butterscotch are ruled by Taurus. Combine the deep kick of coffee ice cream with the salty-sweet taste of butterscotch sauce into a special ice-cream treat. While a sundae every day isn't the best idea for your health, an occasional indulgence is the perfect thing to help you unwind after a long day or treat yourself for a job well done. Taurus responds well to small rewards for her work, so these incentives help establish good routines that will motivate you toward your goals.

Go for a Nature Walk

Taurus's element is earth, which means that her inspiration, drive, and strength come from a deep bond with the great outdoors and all of its beautiful creations. Take a rejuvenating walk through nature—be it on a hiking trail or through a meadow where you can celebrate your connection to Mother Nature with wild flower crowns, observations of various wildlife, and perhaps a few grass stains. When you return to your home and office responsibilities, you'll have the refreshed energy and motivation to tackle any task that comes your way.

Embrace Your Practicality

Sometimes earth signs get a bad reputation for their serious sides, but your practicality is really a positive thing. Earth signs are incredibly sensible and resourceful, and they have a talent for solving problems that others give up on. You come up with real-world solutions that actually work! You love to ponder and thoroughly understand a problem or concept, and like to make charts, graphs, or diagrams to further explore the topic. You stick with a problem through the long haul and come up with a solution that works—celebrate the positives of being the perfect problem-solver!

Take One Step at a Time

S ome people like to jump headfirst into a problem and work it out while trapped in the midst of it. Well that may be great for them, but the thought of it gives earth signs nervous feelings. Earth signs approach almost everything they do with a methodical, step-by-step approach. This method allows you to thoroughly understand exactly what you're getting yourself into, come up with a well-thought-out plan to solve it, and then actually resolve the issue. While it may take you a little more prep time than other people when faced with a problem, you often have a higher success rate too. Breaking down obstacles into clear steps makes earth signs the best problem-solvers around.

Affirm Your Prosperity

A great self-affirmation for Taurus is, "This beautiful earth feeds me." Written down and kept where you can easily come back to it as needed, this phrase serves as a reminder that you are provided for. As an earth sign, Taurus seeks stability and a sense of overall security in her life. Sometimes, though she plans things out and has routines in place, the universe has other plans, and she is left feeling overwhelmed and unsteady on her feet. This affirmation is the perfect comfort that although you may feel out of control, you are taken care of. Change can be a little scary, but you are right where you need to be.

Make Your Home on the Ground Floor

E arth signs instinctually prefer to keep their feet planted firmly on the ground—so their homes should be, as well! Creating a safe, comfortable home is important to earth signs, since it gives them a place to focus on their creative impulses and build a space that's perfect for feeling stable and reenergized.

Ground floor apartments have plenty of perks, such as access to outdoor yard spaces and easier move-in days. And better yet, you'll recharge best in a home where you can easily see (and touch!) the ground. Skip the high-rise apartment, and go for something closer to the first floor instead.

Become a Plant Parent

It should come as no surprise that earth signs find it reassuring to include touches of nature in their homes. Keep yourself centered and relaxed by surrounding yourself with plants. If you're not able to live in a place with easy access to the natural world, try bringing nature to you! City dwellers can plant window boxes or fill their apartments with different types of houseplants.

A window herb garden is a great place to start. Try common herbs like basil, chives, cilantro, oregano, or parsley, which can be great additions to any meal and have many other useful qualities. (Did you know basil is a natural mosquito repellent?) Go all-natural and see how many ways your new garden can benefit your daily life!

Create an Exercise Routine

As a sign that values routine and stability, Taurus is prone to falling into comfortable lethargy— after all, that plush bedspread is oh-so-tempting to this sensual Bull. One way to avoid this tendency and maintain proper care for your physical health is to create an exercise routine. Though getting into a new habit is tricky at first, with a bit of motivation Taurus will quickly become set in a routine.

A simple trick to ensure that you keep at your new exercise schedule is to give yourself small rewards for each victory. Have you worked out every day for the last five days? Treat yourself to a short massage or haircut. Perhaps you have moved up a weight class in your lifting routine. Buy that workout top you've been eying! No matter how small, each step toward better health habits makes a difference.

Save Your Seat

Earth signs are known for seeking stability in their lives—and their work environment is no different. No matter your organizational style or tasks at hand, a sturdy, well-designed office chair is a must-have for any busy earth sign. It isn't easy to get through the workday if you're uncomfortable and distracted. You'll be able to stay focused and work more productively if you're settled at your desk in a chair that's comfortable for you.

Not only will you be better able to concentrate at work, you'll also be taking care of your body. No more stiff necks or backaches for you!

Send Flowers...to Yourself!

No matter the season, earth signs benefit from having plants around. Just like you need plants in your home, you also need some for your office. Especially during dreary rainy days or cold months, you'll need something to reframe your mind-set and spark a positive attitude throughout the day.

Try a monthly flower or plant subscription service to get your plant pick-me-up. Whatever your preference, treat yourself to the perfect desk accessory, with options ranging from handcrafted bouquets to potted plants...or even a succulent or two! No secret admirer is needed—these services will deliver plants of your choice to your desk all year round.

Purchase a Mechanical Bank

Taurus may enjoy the finer things, but she also appreciates the importance of good financial habits. Buy a fun mechanical bank to add a little whimsy to your saving rituals. You'll be motivated to put a bit of money into your savings each month—or even each week—when you hear the satisfying sound of it entering a musical slot, or see it sliding through a sorter, into the chamber below. That extra change, whether it is $1 or $20, adds up. You can also celebrate your celestial roots with a miniature mechanical bull bank.

Soothe Your Throat with Loquat

A small orange fruit grown in Asia, loquat has a number of healing properties, most importantly in soothing the throat. Syrup from the plant is popular in China in cough drops.

Ruler of the throat, Taurus is sensitive to throat-related ailments such as dryness and coughing. Keep loquat cough drops on hand to ward off sore throat during the colder months, so this important channel of Taurean self-expression and communication is open and healthy.

Squeeze a Stuffed Cow

Symbolized by the Bull and ruled by the earth element, Taurus has strong connections to the cow. A plush cow reminds Taurus of her astrological symbol and deep ties to nature. The soft material of a stuffed animal is also comforting to Taurus as she draws understanding of the world around her through her senses—specifically her sense of touch. During times of stress or confusion, giving a cow stuffed animal a squeeze will ground you in the physical world and help you to release those racing thoughts or fears.

Choose Only the Softest Fabrics

E arth signs have a highly developed sense of touch, so choose soft materials for your clothes and sheets. Don't spend your day feeling distracted by an itchy wool sweater or spend all night tossing and turning on scratchy sheets. Restore your healthy skin (and cheerful attitude!) by choosing materials like cashmere, silk, organic cotton, and suede.

You'll prefer any materials or fabrics that touch your skin to be soft and comforting, so go ahead and splurge on high thread count sheets, fluffy towels, and warm, downy blankets.

Take Your Workout Outdoors

As an earth sign, Taurus receives more satisfaction in doing things outdoors. Sensual like her planetary ruler Venus, she wants to feel the wind and sun on her skin, hear different critters scuttling around in the distance, and see all of the colors of Mother Nature's beauty.

One way to encourage Taurus to stick to an exercise routine is to take that workout into nature. Do you usually run on a treadmill or elliptical? Go for a jog on a nature trail or chase your dog around the yard. Do you lift weights? Take them outside! The natural scenery and boost of fresh air may even have you working out longer or more often than before.

Get a Nose Ring

Feeling powerful and a bit adventurous? Get a nose ring. Though the change may seem drastic to steady Taurus, choosing to do something new for herself like getting an eye-catching piercing is the perfect blend of empowerment and control. Choosing a septum nose ring also forges a connection to your symbol, the Bull, which has donned this distinct piercing throughout history. Before you take such a big step, research a good piercer and all the safety guidance on nose rings.

Of course, if you are looking for a less permanent homage to your celestial roots, you can find many rings that do not require piercing, instead using a magnet or a gentle clip to fasten the ring to your nose.

Indulge in Comfort Food

Craving some mac and cheese? A homemade chocolate chip cookie? Maybe even a simple, classic PB&J (peanut butter and jelly)? Reliable earth signs sometimes need to reclaim their roots and find comfort in the well known and well loved.

After a long day indulge in your love of comfort food, whether that's a cheesy slice of pepperoni pizza or a gooey brownie still warm from the oven. Take an uplifting trip down memory lane with simple foods that remind you of your childhood. Enjoyed in moderation, these treats will keep your stomach full and your heart happy.

Find Your Footing
with Green Moss Agate

As an earth sign, Taurus has a special connection to nature. She derives her confidence from having her feet planted firmly on the ground, where she can experience everything through touch, taste, smell, hearing, and sight. Green moss agate is the perfect crystal to help Taurus find and maintain her footing. Smooth and deep green in color, green moss agate will ground you to the earth and create a nurturing vibration that will give you a sense of calm and security.

Treat Your Sweet Tooth

E arth signs are known for their appreciation for the finer things and may enjoy opportunities to indulge. You might find you instinctually gravitate toward sweet flavors. While it's certainly important to eat a balanced diet and enjoy everything in moderation, a sweet treat or two can be just the pick-me-up you need to improve a grumpy mood or curb an unhealthier craving.

Although you may prefer to stick with your reliable, tried-and-true favorites, prevent yourself from becoming "stuck" by looking for your sweet fix in unexpected places. Expand your cultural palate by trying food from different cuisines.

Find Balance for Your Finances

———————————

Self-care isn't always about having fun—sometimes it's simply about that sense of accomplishment you get from checking off a task on your to-do list. Perfect for practical earth signs, make sure to get through those financial day-to-day activities, like reviewing your budget or balancing your checkbook.

Earth signs can be cautious and like to have a sense of security, instead of taking unnecessary risks. A balanced earth sign is able to successfully manage their cautious tendencies and their indulgences. That careful decision-making can help you manage your money well; earth signs have a natural awareness that helps them judge their financial situation exactly. Just make sure you're not obsessing over the task!

Sing!

E very Taurus knows that singing is good for the
soul; in fact, many influential singers are Taurean
(Barbra Streisand, Stevie Wonder, and Adele just to
name a few). Ruler of the throat, Taurus is a sensual
sign who expresses herself through her voice—be it
by talking or singing. Whether you sing karaoke at
a local hangout or take your voice to the stage in a
community production, raise your voice! As you exercise your throat, you'll feel your spirits lift and your
body relax.

Enjoy a Steak

R uled by Venus, Taurus is a sensual sign who enjoys living the high life and pampering her senses. She will delight in savoring a richly seasoned meat such as beef, especially paired with a lovely red wine.

This simple addition to a weekday (or weekend) night is the perfect act of self-care for Taurus, as a tasty meal can release both body and mind of the chaos of the day. As you let go of all of the thoughts, to-dos, and conversations of the past hours, you will be able to properly unwind and restore your warm, earthy energy.

Give Yourself a Time Limit

E arth signs are known for being hard workers;
they're resourceful and know just how to tackle
tasks to make them manageable. They're also notoriously persistent when they're working to achieve their
goals. Being productive and getting things done feels
great to driven earth signs.

Stay on top of your to-do list with this productivity hack! Simply set a time limit with a timer to
get your task done. Since you know you only have a
limited time frame, you'll stay focused, quicken your
pace, and accomplish a lot more than you expected. You'll feel satisfied and proud of all you'll be
able to complete.

Clean with Chamois Cloth

Determined and practical, Taurus enjoys checking things off her to-do list left and right. In fact, a burst of productivity can be just as relaxing to her as a bubble bath. As you move into your household chores, use a chamois cloth to clean your counters, tabletops, and other surfaces. Made from a plush material you will enjoy feeling under your palms, this cloth is natural, durable, and absorbent. It's the perfect environment-friendly and efficient helper—and Taurus does *love* efficiency.

Organize by Color

Ruled by Venus, Taurus is a sensual sign who is deeply affected by the five senses, including sight. Color can have a huge impact on her mood, leading to a day filled with confidence, adaptability, and warmth—or one filled with insecurity, stubbornness, and indifference. Organize your closet by color and season so you are always ready with the best colors for the day—even when you're running a little late for work.

The best colors for Taurus are yellow, pink, and earthy green. Yellow and pink promote creativity, energy, and positive thinking, while green embodies the essence of nature (even when the weather outside is disagreeable). Taurus should avoid red, which signifies anger and obsession. And do not fall into the all-black habit!

Reward Your Patience

In today's fast-paced world, it's important to stay patient, even when lines are slow, orders are misplaced, and Mercury in retrograde causes all kinds of confusion with communication. Luckily, earth signs are known for their ability to stay calm and forgiving. That's a great quality to maintain, so make sure you reward yourself on those days when your patience has been truly tested.

Whether it's enjoying a glass of fine wine, listening to some new music, or splurging on something you've had your eye on for a while, make sure to protect yourself from negativity and do something relaxing and restorative for you and you alone.

Take a Farm Vacation

While some may think Taurus desires only the poshest of posh vacations, her deep connection to the earth and her hardworking nature make a simple farm vacation the perfect rejuvenating experience. Load up your overalls, sunscreen, and a friend or two, and travel to a farm for the weekend.

Between the fresh air, farm animals (say hi to any fellow bulls), and sense of accomplishment if helping out around the property, you'll return home just as satisfied and refreshed as you would after a spa getaway. The ability to share your experience with a friend or loved one—and maybe teach them a thing or two along the way—will make the trip even more memorable.

Dance It Off

You know it's important to take care of your body by exercising. But did you know that earth signs have a good sense of rhythm and may find a new workout routine through dancing? It's also a great way to add fun into an existing exercise schedule or try something new so your usual routine doesn't get boring.

Try a peaceful ballet class for discipline, or experiment with jazz and hip-hop for a fun, high-energy workout. Or look for other dance-inspired classes like Zumba or barre, which combine dance elements and workout styles for unique and challenging programs.

Enjoy the Power of Music

Earth signs love music. When you're feeling stressed, try using music to relax yourself. If you find yourself in a difficult situation, try to take a break to re-center and calm down. Put on your headphones, and let the sound of the music soothe you and distract you from your worries. Experiment with different genres to see what works best for you.

You may even find it relaxing to do some singing yourself—even if it's only in the safety of your own shower!

Grow Your Own Vegetables

I f you live in an area with a backyard or communal space—or even if you live in a studio apartment with a kitchen window—try your hand at growing vegetables. In a larger space, you can plant rows of different vegetables, while in a smaller apartment space you can grow a pot of herbs or hang a bucket with tomato plants in direct sunlight.

Seeing Mother Nature's creations flourish firsthand will give you an even deeper appreciation of her power—plus you will have a healthy, pesticide-free treat to enjoy right from the pot or mixed into a homemade meal.

Add a Soundtrack to
Your Daily Chores

Sometimes, chores get to be boring and stressful for even the most practical and grounded of earth signs. And whether it's breaking out the vacuum cleaner or dusting every horizontal surface in your home, everyone has that one task that seems so unpleasant and difficult to finish.

For earth signs this is the perfect time to turn to your love of music to keep yourself mentally alert and refocus yourself on the task at hand. Whistling while completing your everyday tasks will keep you relaxed and help you tackle even your least favorite chores with ease.

Decorate with Pink Cyclamen

Add a bit of Mother Earth's bounty to your décor! Sturdy, much like Taurus, pink cyclamen is a lovely pink flower that also serves as a reminder of nature's tough but delicate beauty. Pink is also a Taurus power color, and a vase of pink cyclamen in a living or office space will boost energy and creativity. To care for your plant, ensure that it receives plenty of indirect sunlight. Cyclamen also requires a humid atmosphere, so spray the leaves with water at any sign of dryness.

Balance Your Element

As an earth sign, Taurus enjoys routines and planning. She rarely steps out of the house without a schedule and a clear vision of her goals for the day. While her ambitious, thoughtful nature is one of the things that makes her so impressive, sometimes this need for routine can lead her to become stagnant in her progress or resistant to change of any kind.

Balance out your earthy side with an airy dose of spontaneity. This can be as simple as hopping on your bike for a quick ride around the block when you were planning to recline in front of the TV. Whatever you do, do it on a whim. This rejuvenating experience is sure to clear out any stagnant energy.

Train for a Marathon

Patient earth signs are in it for the long haul; their workout style is more marathon than sprint. These slow and steady athletes are disciplined and committed to achieving their goals.

Your body will thank you for taking on activities like running, biking, dancing, or even jump roping! You may even want to train to run a marathon, or participate in a triathlon, which will really test your endurance with a series of swimming, biking, and running challenges. These activities will keep you feeling refreshed and rejuvenated, while helping you develop strength and stamina.

Go for the Goal!

I f you're looking for a team sport, keep in mind the
earth signs' tendencies to look for ways to use
their strength and stamina. Try sports like soccer or
volleyball that combine those skills. With team sports
like these, you'll be able to take care of your body
and develop strong, supportive friendships, all while
having the added benefit of keeping your feet in your
comfort zone...firmly on the ground.

Your endurance will keep you going from the
beginning of the game to the very last second. And
your goal-oriented nature is sure to keep you on the
winning team as you help your team toward victory!

Treat Your Palate to an Indian Specialty

As a sign ruled by sensual Venus, Taurus has quite the refined palate. The right blend of tastes can make her senses come alive, lifting her mood and leaving her revitalized. This chutney is the perfect flavor to delight this epicurean Bull as it mixes the spicy tastes of red pepper, ginger, and mustard seeds with the sweet flavors of raisins and sugar to create a sauce that goes perfectly with cheeses, meat, and more.

To make mango chutney, simply bring the following ingredients to a boil: 2 cups sugar and 1 cup distilled white vinegar. Next, add the following ingredients, reduce to a simmer, and cook for 1 hour: 6 cups cubed fresh mangoes, 1 cup chopped sweet onion, ½ cup golden raisins, ¼ cup finely chopped ginger, 1 garlic clove (minced), 1 teaspoon whole brown mustard seeds, and ¼ teaspoon red chili pepper flakes (if you desire an extra kick). Enjoy!

Try a Stress-Free Workout

If the thought of running a marathon has you sweating already, don't worry! There are other workouts perfect for earth signs, like learning to work on a balance bar or taking some beginners' gymnastics skills classes. With your disciplined attitude, you'll be able to focus on improving your strength and stability while mastering these challenging skills.

This workout can be a great way to take care of your body and keep it healthy and toned. But it can also be a much-needed opportunity to relax and compose yourself on an otherwise busy day. The focus you'll need to master carefully controlled movements will help take your mind off the stress of your day and give you a chance to recharge.

Meditate On Your Mantra

Taurus is rooted firmly on the ground. As a fixed earth sign, she values stability and careful planning. However, life can have things in store for Taurus that she may not expect. A powerful mantra for Taurus to meditate on during these uncertain times is, "I am secure in all parts of my life."

As you come across surprises that may shake your Taurean confidence, reciting this mantra will allow you to ground yourself back in reality and meditate on the stability you do have in both your surroundings and your own character. A good place to begin is to sit in the lotus pose with your eyes closed. Then, quietly chant the mantra out loud. The rhythmic sounds alone will soon draw in a feeling of calm.

Stretch Your Workout Routine

E arth signs enjoy having an established routine they can count on, so try developing a well-rounded workout routine that works for you. Add stretching as a consistent part of your routine to keep you feeling strong and healthy. Stretching can also prevent more serious injuries throughout your workout. Since stretching keeps your muscles flexible and relaxed, it's a perfect release if you're feeling stiff from a long day in the office, or even just tense and stressed. This easy, revitalizing addition to your workouts will make your body feel great.

Curl Up with a Book

———————

P art of Taurus's ability to express herself lies in her talent for reflection. With her keen senses and an emotional intelligence that comes with being ruled by the planet of love (Venus), Taurus is able to uncover things about herself and the outside world through her observations. A great way to facilitate further reflection is by reading books. Make yourself comfortable with a soft blanket on the couch and crack open a book by a fellow Taurus. Taurean authors include Shakespeare, Charlotte Brontë, and Harper Lee.

Energize with the "Toreador Song"

A sign that knows just how to stimulate the senses, Taurus is the queen of relaxation. Sometimes, however, this leisure can pull her into a place of over-stimulation or lethargy. When Taurus has overridden her senses, she becomes overwhelmed and insecure, while a numbing of the senses due to overindulgence leaves her unmotivated.

To kick-start inspiration and provide that much-needed boost of energy, play the "Toreador Song" from Bizet's opera *Carmen*. Not only is this classic aria a wonderful blend of musical talent and enthusiasm, but it is also connected to Taurus's astrological symbol, the Bull. It's the perfect Taurus theme song!

Use Yoga to Recharge

Working out is all about finding the right balance. Try mixing your weights and cardio with yoga stretches to keep muscles limber. Think yoga isn't right for you? Don't worry—there are many different styles and class types, so you'll be able to find the perfect, restorative approach that's right for you and your body's needs.

By adding yoga into your routine, you may find yourself becoming stronger and more flexible. But your brain will also benefit by getting a break from thinking, worrying, and stressing. Since it's important to focus your awareness on your body and concentrate on performing each pose as best you can, you'll find your worries can take a back seat while you recharge.

Look Before You Leap

E arth signs are logica l thinkers, who often like
to fully evaluate their options before making
a decision. They're seeking safety and security, so
they aren't interested in taking big risks. Taking that
essential time to think things through can be a major
benefit for their mental health. You certainly don't
want to be rushed into making a decision!

If you find yourself faced with a problem or challenging situation, think it over privately before confid-
ing in a friend. Give yourself permission to reclaim the
time and space you need for yourself. You'll feel more
confident sharing your decisions and more comfortable moving forward.

Simplify Your Work Wardrobe

Although Taurus can delight in a luxe ensemble, she has many places to be and people to see—and a simple wardrobe is key. Having a few pieces that you can mix and match makes weekday mornings run much smoother, an efficiency that every Taurus appreciates. Besides, Taurus prefers to channel her creativity into better things like food and the arts. Invest in items that are easy to maintain and go with everything, like wrinkle-free tops and pants or skirts in neutral and pastel colors.

Meditate in Nature

It's important to take a few moments to yourself to relax, refresh, and gather your thoughts. To get some peace of mind, try meditating in nature. Particularly for thoughtful earth signs, this time-out ritual can be helpful to clear your mind.

One option is to find a comfortable seated position, close your eyes, and focus on your breathing and the present moment before allowing yourself to pay attention to the natural world around you. Or try meditating while walking and see how nature interacts with each of your senses. What sounds can you hear? What are you able to touch? How does your body feel? Earth signs may find it particularly helpful to meditate on the flowers and trees around them.

Reduce Stress with Grounding

It's no surprise that earth signs should be in close contact with the earth itself. One way to literally connect with the earth is to try "grounding," or standing or walking barefoot outside on the grass, soil, or sand. Not only does being barefoot outside just feel good, it may also reduce stress and inflammation while improving your circulation and mood. Try to spend 30 minutes a day grounding—either all at once or broken up into smaller chunks of time. Afterward, you'll find yourself relaxed, restored, and recharged.

Keep a Treasure Chest

Reflective Taurus draws wisdom about herself and the world around her by looking back at past experiences. Her planetary ruler, Venus, also governs romantic feelings, making Taurus a sentimental sign. Keep a "treasure chest" of mementos from the past, including photos and other reminders of fond times, to pull out whenever you are in need of a little trip down memory lane.

Has an unexpected change occurred in your life? These keepsakes will lift your spirits and help you feel more grounded. Unsure why your boss chose you for a big project? The mementos of your past accomplishments will serve as a wonderful reminder that you are hardworking and capable—*of course* the boss picked you!

Go Forest Bathing

J ust like regular bathing involves immersing yourself in water, forest bathing is the process of immersing yourself in trees and nature. The Environmental Protection Agency recently found that the average American spends 93 percent of their time indoors, but earth signs especially benefit from regular contact with Mother Earth.

Forest bathing is an easy, relaxing way to enjoy the outdoors. Silence your devices so you savor your senses—see the various shades of green, smell the various flowers, feel the crisp air, and listen to the crunch of branches under your feet.

Slip Into a Silky Secret

Ruled by sensual Venus, Taurus experiences the world around her through heightened senses. One of the most important of her senses is that of touch. Touch is what allows Taurus to truly savor her surroundings, especially as a sign who appreciates the plush side of life. The feel of silk underwear in a Taurus color such as yellow, pink, or green will be a secret delight.

These colors will promote confidence and renewed energy for your day, while the soft fabric will help you to unwind once your work is finished.

Declutter Your Home
and Your Mind

Earth signs are known to hang onto too many belongings. While you may enjoy the memories that these items bring, keeping too many of them will eventually clutter your physical and mental space.

Take a day to go through your possessions and decide what's most meaningful to you. If an item has outlasted its usefulness to you, donate it to someone who would enjoy it more. When you've finished, take notice of the physical space you've created and meditate in or near it for a few minutes if possible. You'll likely find that you've also freed up mental space for new ideas.

Detox with a Mud Mask

After a long day, nothing feels better than a relaxing facial mask. And what better type for an earth sign than a mud mask? Clear away the pollutants and bacteria your face is exposed to on a daily basis using an element of the earth itself.

If time and your budget allow, you can visit a spa for a mud mask—but if that's not possible, pick one up at a drugstore or natural foods store and apply it yourself at home, taking slow, deep breaths as you let the mixture sit on your face. You'll find this detox to be especially restorative and cleansing.

Cook with Copperware

Shiny and rich in color, it is no surprise that copper is ruled by Venus, the planet in charge of beauty. Copper cookware is not just beautiful—it is also very useful and efficient. Though she does admire style, Taurus is a down-to-earth sign who chooses utility over physical appeal. With copperware you can have both—and a delicious meal. (Be sure to choose copperware with a nonreactive lining, or follow the manufacturer's instructions for safe use.) A mixture of table salt and white wine vinegar, rinsed off with water, will keep your copperware shining like new.

Learn a Circle Dance

In many cultures circle dances are a tradition that celebrates the earth and connects a group of people together through both physical touch and music. With her sensitive ears and appreciation for the arts, Taurus loves both music and dance. She is also an earth sign, drawing energy and confidence from her connection with Mother Nature. It is important, too, for Taurus to exercise her rhythm and coordination regularly, as she rules over the cerebellum—the part of the body that controls motor function.

You can find information online about where to learn a traditional circle dance, or you can use online videos to teach yourself. Share what you've learned at your next friend gathering, and get a circle dance going! All you'll need is a little music to set the mood.

Paint a Rock

Earth signs like to be crafty, so let your creativity shine by painting a symbol of the earth—a rock! Head outdoors to find a few suitable rocks—usually, flat, smooth ones are the easiest canvas. You might want to start by painting a base layer of white paint so other colors show up better. Add details or hand lettering with fine-tip permanent markers.

Let the experience be quiet and meditative—listen to ambient music as you paint. When your design is complete, cover it with a clear coat of Mod Podge (following the directions) to seal it in. You can keep the rock for yourself as a reminder of your connection to the earth, or pass along its good energy and give it as a gift to a friend or loved one.

Set a New Goal for Yourself

Many people use the start of a new year to set goals. But there's no need to wait for January 1 to do that. As an earth sign, you'll benefit from setting a practical goal for yourself, and then tracking your progress, no matter what time of year it is. Whether you're trying to get rid of a bad habit or institute a healthy new one, setting a goal and noting checkpoints along the way makes you much more likely to be successful.

When you think of a goal, write it down and post it in a place where you'll see it frequently. Be sure to reward yourself every time you meet one of your checkpoints to keep yourself motivated.

Treat Yourself to
New Loungewear

Everyone owns some favorite sweats or comfy shirts. But many of us wear this loungewear until it's ripped, stretched out, and stained. Take stock of what you currently own and see if some of it can be recycled or donated. Then treat yourself to some new items, and enjoy them the next time you're unwinding at home after a long day in less-than-comfortable work clothes.

Earth signs love to be comfortable, so repeat this process once a year. You'll look forward to relaxing and recharging in your new pieces!

Opt for Honey

Natural and delicious, pure honey is the perfect alternative to artificial sweeteners (as long as you are not allergic to bees or bee products). Raw honey also contains a number of healthy properties, including antioxidants that can lower blood pressure, improve cholesterol levels, and reduce the risk of heart disease. You will still feel like you are indulging, even when you are making a healthier choice!

Honey can also soothe sore throats and coughing, which is important for Taurus, as she rules the throat. A sore throat can mean difficulty in self-expression and communication with others—two things that are crucial to Taurus's well-being.

Create a Personal Spa

Taurus is known for her dedication to her work. Just like her astrological symbol, the Bull, she perseveres through any obstacles that may arise, and gets the job done. It is important for Taurus to unwind after her hard work, and give her senses a chance to refresh. Without proper self-care, she can become stuck in a place of stress and sensory overload, so this relaxation is crucial to her well-being. Create a spa-like atmosphere in your home to release the events of the day. Simple accents such as candles that cast a mellow light and soft music will be just the ticket to a renewed you.

Talk It Out

Taurus is ruled by Venus, the planet of love. Sometimes, Taurus may become overwhelmed by her feelings or view them as a roadblock to getting things done. In these times, her emotions can be pushed to the wayside, where they only grow. Instead of bottling your emotions and wishing they would just disappear, talk to someone.

This person can be a counselor, or even family member. Whoever you choose, you will find that the people around you are ready and willing to listen and return all of your Taurean compassion and loyalty. As you release your emotions, you will feel any stress or negative thoughts you were carrying lift away, creating the space for your creativity and sense of security to return.

Try Aromatherapy

Earth signs are closely in touch with all of their senses. Aromatherapy is a simple and easy way for you to connect with and savor your sense of smell. You can enjoy a citrus body wash to energize yourself during your morning shower, sip some ginger tea to recharge in a midafternoon slump, read in a room scented by a soothing vanilla candle, or spritz (diluted according to instructions) lavender essential oil on your pillow before bed to relax.

When you begin practicing aromatherapy regularly, you'll find yourself more in tune with your sense of smell all the time. You'll notice the scent of your neighbor's flowers, the mixture of flavors wafting from your favorite restaurant, and the earthy smells after a spring rain.

Volunteer for an
Environmental Cause

Donating your time and effort to a cause you're passionate about is a great way to show you care about the world around you—and yourself. After all, research shows that people who volunteer are less stressed, have more friends, and are more confident! As an earth sign, honor your connection to the planet by volunteering for a group that protects the environment, reduces pollution, encourages people to get outside, or safeguards animals.

There are many ways to help, including performing manual labor, organizing fundraising, and offering skills like bookkeeping or web design. You will feel fulfilled and proud—and your work will be making a difference.

Make Your Own Jewelry

As an earth sign, Taurus loves working with her hands, creating something from start to finish that she can then use in her daily life. One great hobby for Taurus to pursue is jewelry making! You can find aisles of different tools, instructions, and elements to create your own bracelets, earrings, and more at your local craft store. Go for metals, wood beads, and colors of nature that remind you of your celestial element. The sense of satisfaction (and unique new fashion statement) in making your own jewelry will lift your spirits and reconnect you with your earthy roots.

Get Outside!

L ying on the couch after work might have become routine for you, but what if you switched your habit? Earth signs are prone to becoming lethargic, so try to get outside for a walk almost every evening after you eat.

Walking will aid digestion, help you stay fit, and encourage you to decompress and unwind in a healthy way. Vary your route periodically to keep the walk from getting boring. An evening stroll is also a great way to engage with your community—say hi to people you walk by, buy lemonade from a kids' stand, or even join in a pickup basketball game.

Visit a Farmers' Market

Farmers' markets offer an astounding array of local produce and homemade foods. You might be surprised at what's being grown right around you. There's sure to be a market in your area—find out its schedule and pop in regularly. Let your senses savor the offerings—see the brightly colored displays, smell the fresh peaches and herbs, and maybe snag a sample bite that a stall is offering. Look for organic produce, which is good for the environment and your health.

Try to find recipes that use your farmers' market haul for a couple of dinners a week, and grab the whole fruits for easy snacks on the go.

Wrap Yourself in Turkish Cotton

R uled by sensual Venus and the earth element, Taurus experiences life through her keen senses of sight, hearing, taste, smell, and especially touch. The different textures she encounters impact how she perceives her surroundings, and a pleasurable fabric is the perfect accoutrement for allowing her to relax and recharge. Wrap yourself in a warm Turkish towel after a shower or exercise, and you'll soon find your imagination roaming to a luxurious getaway. Once restored, you will be ready for whatever work project or creative venture you have planned.

Invite Financial Success

Taurus is a hardworking, practical sign who knows the importance of managing finances wisely. Magnetize financial prosperity with a beautiful and useful wallet. This wallet can be compact for your travels—or the latest trend—but make sure it has all of the necessary slots and zippers for securely holding your possessions. Try finding one in one of the Taurus power colors: pink, yellow, or green. Pink and yellow encourage positivity and abundance, while green promotes security.

Live It Up on Weekdays!

There's no need to wait for a weekend to go out for dinner or a night on the town! As an earth sign, you probably enjoy structure and routine, but you don't want to fall into ruts either. To avoid that, shake things up and enjoy a concert on a Monday evening, head out to dinner at a new restaurant on a Tuesday night, or go dancing on Wednesday after work. You'll release any stress you've been holding onto and take the pressure off your weekends to supply *every* bit of fun in your life.

Invest Your Money

———————

Earth signs are conscientious—money matters tend to come easy for you. Still, you want to be sure that your money isn't just sitting in an account somewhere. Put it to work for you by making wise investments.

Do some research with trusted sources to be sure your investments are smart, and work with a broker or on your own to make the actual transactions. Check in periodically to see how your accounts are doing and make adjustments as needed. Over time, your investments will grow and you'll enjoy even more fortune.

Savor a Fruity Tea

Taurus is known for having a sensitive palate due to her planetary ruler, Venus. Fruit-flavored teas such as mango, raspberry, and peach delight Taurus's taste buds while promoting calm—and wellness too. The sweet flavors of the tea may have you feeling like you are indulging, but you are actually sipping on quite the healthy treat! Fruity teas boast a number of wonderful health-giving properties, including antioxidants and improved digestion. Tea has also been shown to promote weight loss, prevent cavities, and reduce the risk of heart disease. Drink up!

Do a Waltz

Taurus loves to dance, but it may come as a surprise that it is also important to her well-being. As the ruler of the cerebellum, which controls balance and motor function, it is essential for Taurus to practice moving fluidly and matching a rhythm. The waltz is a soothing rhythm that will allow you to release any tensions from the day and exercise your coordination. Try dancing to the "Blue Danube" waltz, which is sure to leave you feeling confident and upbeat.

Spring for an Expensive Bottle of Wine

L ife is too short to drink inexpensive wine *all* the time. Every once in a while, treat yourself to an expensive, high-quality bottle of wine. As an earth sign, you can appreciate the finer things in life, and you have a great sense of taste. Ask an employee at your local liquor store for a recommendation based on your preferences, or reach for a longtime favorite of yours.

Take out your nice glassware, let the bottle breathe, and then swirl and sip slowly so you can really taste the subtle notes in the glass as you relax and unwind.

Duet with a Fellow Taurean

M usic is for Taurus's ears what food is for her taste buds. Sensitive and expressive like her planetary ruler, Venus, Taurus uses music as an outlet for her creativity and emotions. Connect with your inner performer with a "duet." True, you may be in the shower with a Bluetooth speaker, or in your living room with a karaoke machine, but singing along with a fellow Taurus is an empowering act of self-care that will leave you feeling inspired and more confident than ever. Talented Taurus singers include Roy Orbison (try his fan favorite "Oh, Pretty Woman") and Kelly Clarkson.

Try to Compromise

Earth signs have so many wonderful qualities, but one characteristic that might trouble you sometimes is your stubbornness. Instead of getting down on yourself, turn that trait around by consciously working to compromise whenever possible.

For example, if a friend wants to go out to one type of restaurant and you want another, talk for a few minutes to determine someplace you'd both like. If your partner prefers one couch but you want to buy another, work out a solution based on what's best for your space. These types of thoughtful, caring conversations go a long way toward ensuring harmony in your relationships.

Create Your Own Pottery

You've probably seen gorgeous pottery in stores, but have you ever tried to make it yourself? For a fun activity, work with some clay to make your own creation, be it a simple bowl, a mug for your morning coffee, or a decoration to give as a gift. Earth signs are in touch with their senses, and this hands-on craft allows you to get your hands dirty and really savor your sense of touch.

Take a class at a local art center or craft store where you can make a piece from start to finish. Once you've made your creation, you can have it fired by the professionals in its natural color or painted.

Restore Inner Peace with Coral

Are you at a point in your life where things seem to constantly be shifting? Wear a pink coral necklace (or another piece of jewelry containing pink coral) that you can rub between your fingers when needed. A natural element of the sea, coral encourages balance during times of change. And just as the ocean is full of unpredictable movement, so is life. However, there is calm between the waves, and the ocean is a steady force capable of weathering any storm.

As a fixed sign ruled by the earth element, Taurus values stability, and can become overwhelmed or headstrong in the face of change. Coral jewelry will serve as a reminder that like the ocean, you are steady, and you have the strength to weather these changes in your life.

Daydream to Calm Your Mind

In today's world it's easy to have your brain running nonstop. Work, family, and other responsibilities are on your mind—you probably jump from one practical thought to the next with no break. It's time to change that and give your head a break!

Allow yourself time to daydream about something positive every day—whether it's while you shower in the morning, during your lunch break, or before you go to bed. Banish thoughts of bills or deadlines and think of something wonderful—a favorite vacation spot, a warm memory with a loved one, or a life goal you're trying to achieve. You'll find this practice leaves you mentally energized, refreshed, and balanced.

Whip Up a Delicious
Green Smoothie

Feeling tired, hungry, and de-energized during a late afternoon slump? Instead of overindulging in an unhealthy snack you eat mindlessly, restore yourself with a smoothie made with fresh, leafy greens from the earth. Kale, arugula, and spinach are good sources of folate, fiber, and vitamins A and C, plus they are filled with antioxidants and are known to improve heart health.

Grab one at a juice bar near you, or make your own, adding chunks of pear, honey, or apple to the greens to create a bit of sweetness in your drink. Savor each sip, and notice how it makes you feel restored and rejuvenated with no guilt!

Strike a Plow Pose

The Plow Pose is the perfect yoga position for Taurus, as it connects her to her astrological symbol, the Bull. This is not a beginner's pose, so make sure to practice this with your yoga instructor for technique guidance. To do this pose, lie flat on your back with your arms at your sides. Breath in, and lift your legs and hips up (using your hands to support your lower back) toward the ceiling. Straighten your legs and slowly lower your toes to the floor behind your head. Be sure to keep a space between your chin and chest. Gaze downward and hold for a few seconds. Then gently roll out of the position.

Go for a Picnic

Picnicking wraps nature and your favorite indulgences into one sweet little package of self-care. As an earth sign, Taurus has a special connection to nature, which explains why one of the best ways for her to unwind and renew her creative spirit is through a bit of one-on-one time with Mother Nature. Taurus is also the queen of luxury, as her keen Venusian senses give her one truly refined palate.

Choose a warm afternoon to pack up a basket with your favorite foods and go on a picnic. Be sure to find a location with plenty of trees and wildlife, and you'll soon find yourself released from any stress or worry that may have been weighing you down.

Indulge in a Day Off

Earth signs are very practical and dependable, but they can take that dedication too far and end up overworking themselves. Treat yourself to days off from work or life periodically to recharge your batteries. A mental health day can do wonders for your happiness, creativity, and health.

Be sure to take the whole day to relax—don't fill it up with errands and appointments. Go for a long walk outside, enjoy a coffee at a local café, take a warm bath... Spend your time focusing on what your body needs to restore itself—you deserve it!

Toast with Planter's Punch

A colorful beach-day favorite, planter's punch is the perfect elixir for Taurus after a long week of hard work. Originating in South Carolina, planter's punch mixes refreshing citrusy flavors with rich dark rum. To create this fruity concoction, simply fill a glass with ice and mix in the following ingredients: 1½ ounces dark rum, ½ ounce lime juice, 1 ounce pineapple juice, ½ ounce orange juice, and ¼ ounce simple syrup. Garnish with an orange slice and a maraschino cherry, and enjoy your ticket to paradise.

Take a Trip to a Museum

Creative and refined, Taurus has a deep appreciation for the arts. Travel to an art museum and feel your own inspiration grow, as you explore paintings and sculptures by famous artists. Taurus artists on display in many museums include Salvador Dalí, Tamara de Lempicka, and Keith Haring.

You can also pay homage to your celestial symbol by visiting a famous piece of art inspired by the Bull. One painting created by esteemed Italian artist Titian depicts the popular Greek myth of Zeus and Europa. In this myth, Zeus transforms into a white bull and carries the maiden Europa, the inspiration for the name of the continent of Europe, to the island of Crete.

Aim for the Bull's Eye

Ruled by sensual Venus, Taurus is a very tactile sign. Just thinking about her goals and imagining them coming to fruition isn't going to be enough. Taurus needs to see and feel her hard work paying off. Create this motivational visual aid by making your own bull's eye target. In the center of the target, write down a goal you are working toward. If your progress has stalled, or you are in need of a boost of encouragement in pursuing your dreams, you can take aim and throw bean bags at your target. You can also celebrate an achievement with a satisfying bean bag toss at the bull's eye. Once you have reached one goal, write in a new one, aim, and fire away!

Talk to a Friend

These days we often rely on texting to keep in touch with friends. While that's a good method a lot of the time, it's also vital to keep friendships strong by talking on the phone or, even better, in person. Earth signs are very loyal, and your friends are important to you. Show them that by prioritizing them in your schedule. Find time to catch up so you can move past emojis and nurture the type of close bond you and your friend deserve.

If finding a mutually agreeable time is proving difficult, get creative—for example, take a walk or jog together so you can exercise *and* catch up.

Ease Into Sleep with Silk

Having trouble falling asleep? Cover your pillow in a peach-colored silk pillowcase. The silk fabric feels sensuous and won't leave wrinkles on your face. Ruled by Venus, Taurus is especially sensitive to texture, so a rough material on her pillowcase will make it more difficult to fall and stay asleep. Silk will feel amazing on your skin, and a restful sleep will make all the difference tomorrow when you are tackling your to-do list.

Taurus is also sensitive to color, so a brightly colored pillowcase will make it hard to wind down for the night. Peach is a soft, welcoming color that promotes calm, so you will feel relaxed and ready for dreamland.

Boost Your Mood with Jasmine

It is no secret that life is full of surprises. Though Taurus would prefer warning of a month—or year—before these changes. Steady and headstrong like a bull, Taurus can lose her footing when the unexpected happens, but don't fear. If you are feeling less than your confident Taurean self, jasmine essential oil is the perfect way to naturally lift your spirits.

Boasting subtly sweet notes, jasmine has an uplifting effect that can help you shake any insecure feelings brought on by change. It also promotes restful sleep and healthy skin! You can diffuse jasmine essential oil in a living or sleeping space or massage it (diluted according to instructions) into your skin.

About the Author

Constance Stellas is an astrologer of Greek heritage with more than twenty-five years of experience. She primarily practices in New York City and counsels a variety of clients, including business CEOs, artists, and scholars. She has been interviewed by *The New York Times*, *Marie Claire*, and *Working Woman*, and has appeared on several New York TV morning shows, featuring regularly on Sirius XM and other national radio programs as well. Constance is the astrologer for *HuffPost* and a regular contributor to Thrive Global. She is also the author of several titles, including *The Astrology Gift Guide*, *Advanced Astrology for Life*, *The Everything® Sex Signs Book*, and the graphic novel series Tree of Keys, as well as coauthor of *The Hidden Power of Everyday Things*. Learn more about Constance at her website, ConstanceStellas.com, or on *Twitter* (@Stellastarguide).